World's Boldest Engineer

Emily

(your name)

Draw a picture of yourself here!

THE STORY OF ROSIE REVERE, ENGINEER

Rosie Revere is a shy second grader in Miss Lila Greer's classroom at Blue River Creek. She dreams of becoming a great engineer, but she never lets anyone know about her dreams.

When Rosie was young, she made amazing inventions for her uncles and aunts. Everyone loved her inventions.

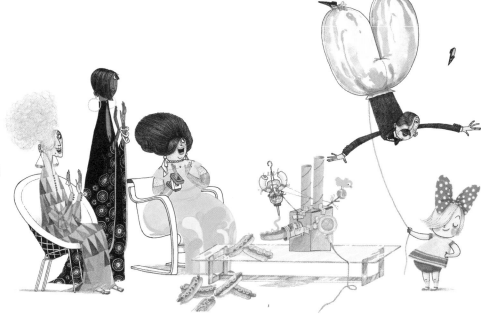

Nobody loved them more than her uncle, Zookeeper Fred. Rosie invented a special hat for keeping snakes off his head. She used parts of a fan and some cheddar-cheese spray (which everyone knows keeps pythons away). Uncle Fred loved it so much that he couldn't contain his joy. He burst out laughing! He laughed so hard that he slapped his knee and his eyes filled with tears.

But Rosie misunderstood. She thought that he was laughing at her, and it broke her heart. Perhaps she couldn't become an engineer after all. From that day, Rosie kept her inventions—and her dreams—to herself.

When Rosie was in second grade, her great-great-aunt came for a visit. Her name was Rose. Great-Great-Aunt Rose told Rosie about all the amazing things she had done in her life. She had had many thrills and had even built enormous airplanes to help her country.

Great-Great-Aunt Rose had done lots of exciting things, but there was one thing left on her list of adventures: She wanted to fly. But now that she was old, she didn't think she would ever get the chance.

That night, Rosie tried to sleep, but she couldn't. She kept thinking about Great-Great-Aunt Rose. Rosie wondered if she could create a gizmo to help her aunt fly. But when she thought about Uncle Fred's cheese hat, she felt sad.

"No," she thought, "I can't help."

3

However, some questions are tricky, and this one would not let go of Rosie. It kept her awake all night, and when morning came, she knew just how to make her aunt fly. She worked and worked and worked. Finally, at the end of the day, she was done. Rosie dragged her invention onto the lawn to give it a test and see if it would be a ridiculous flop.

Rosie climbed into the cockpit. She flipped on the switch. The heli-o-cheese-copter shuddered and shook. It lunged and lurched. It whirled around and around in the air. Then it froze for a heartbeat and—CRASH!—it hit the ground.

Rosie heard someone laughing and wheezing. It was Great-Great-Aunt Rose, who slapped her knee and laughed so hard that her eyes filled with tears. Just like Uncle Fred! Rosie's heart was broken all over again, and she knew that she would never be a great engineer.

Rosie turned around to leave, but Great-Great-Aunt Rose hugged her tight and kissed her.

"You did it! Hurray!" she said. "It's the perfect first try!"

Rosie did not understand. "It crashed," she said. "The heli-o-cheese-copter failed!"

"Of course!" said her great-great-aunt. "Your brilliant first flop was a raging success! I can't wait for the next one. Let's get working!"

Then she gave young Rosie a notebook and pencil, and it all became clear. Life might have its failures, but failing is just part of learning. The only true failure can come if you quit.

Great-Great-Aunt Rose tied her headscarf around Rosie's head and they worked together until it was time for bed. And when she slept, Rosie Revere dreamed the bold dreams of a great engineer.

Rosie collects all kinds of things for her inventions.
Here are some things she finds useful.
She calls these items her "ENGINEER'S TREASURE."
You might find them useful, too.

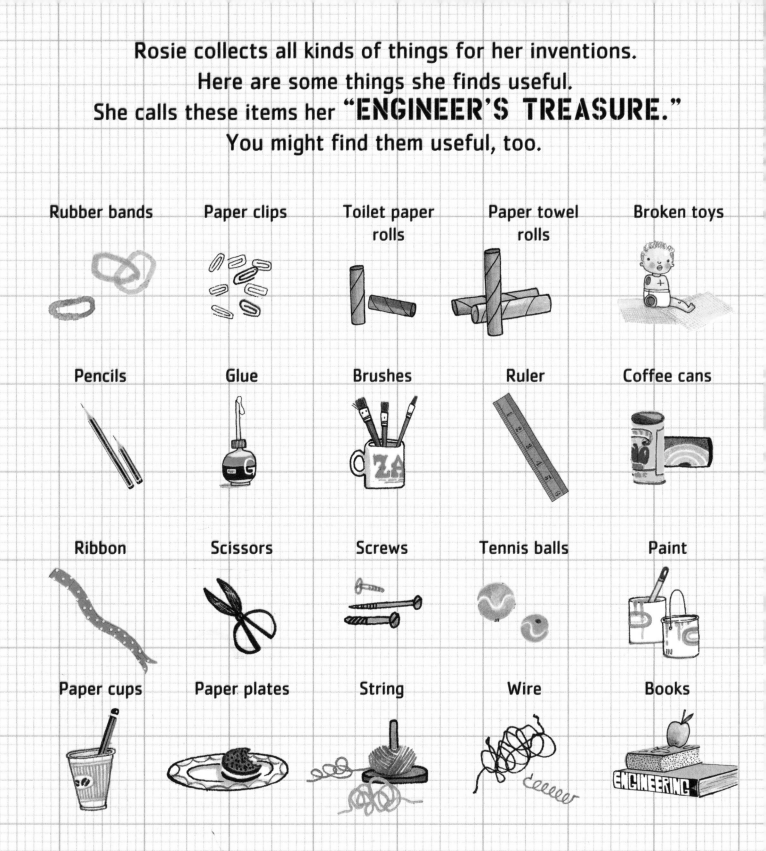

Rubber bands — Paper clips — Toilet paper rolls — Paper towel rolls — Broken toys

Pencils — Glue — Brushes — Ruler — Coffee cans

Ribbon — Scissors — Screws — Tennis balls — Paint

Paper cups — Paper plates — String — Wire — Books

Tape—There are lots of kinds of helpful tape, including: duct tape, packing tape, double-sided tape, Scotch tape, painter's tape, masking tape, and gaffer tape. Each has its own use.

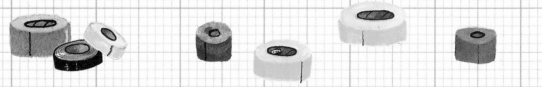

Where can **you** find ENGINEER'S TREASURE?

There are many places you can find cool things to use in your inventions.

- RECYCLING: Cardboard boxes, broken toys, juice cans, milk jugs, plastic lids, and other things your family might otherwise throw away. Ask permission and make sure they're clean and safe to use.
- RUMMAGE SALES and THRIFT MARKETS are great places to find useful items inexpensively. Finding a new use for something old keeps it out of the landfill!
- SWAP treasure with your engineering friends.
- If you can't find a recycled thing to use, you might find something at a HARDWARE STORE or a FABRIC STORE.

AND BE CAREFUL WHEN WORKING WITH SHARP TOOLS OR BROKEN PIECES! MAKE SURE AN ADULT IS ALWAYS NEARBY!

MORE ITEMS FROM AN ENGINEER'S TOOLBOX: (USE ONLY WITH AN ADULT'S PERMISSION)

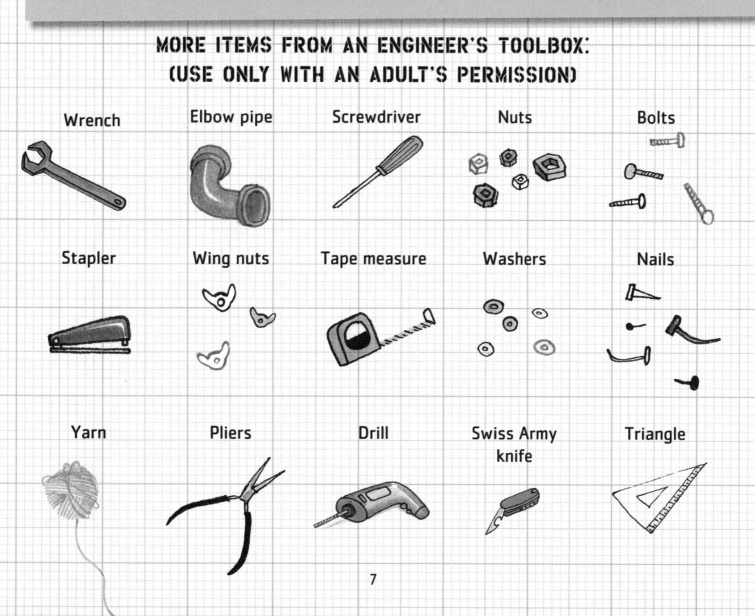

Wrench   Elbow pipe   Screwdriver   Nuts   Bolts

Stapler   Wing nuts   Tape measure   Washers   Nails

Yarn   Pliers   Drill   Swiss Army knife   Triangle

KEEP YOUR ENGINEER'S TREASURE ORGANIZED!

Treasure is all around. But not everything is a treasure.
Choose items that are safe, clean, and useful.
A good collection has variety and is well organized.

Organizing your tools and treasure . . .

* keeps them in good shape, so they last longer.

* lets you find what you need when you need it.

* saves money because you don't have to replace things you already have.

* keeps your space free so you can make things.

* keeps your feet free of holes!

HERE ARE SOME TIPS:

* Decorate and label empty shoeboxes to store under your bed or on a shelf.

* Keep similar things together.

* Small, clean glass jars with lids make great containers for tiny parts like screws and bolts or supplies like rubber bands and string. Clear jars let you easily see what you have!

* A clear plastic shoe holder over the back of a door keeps things organized and easily viewed.

* Hang tools or spools of ribbon on hooks on a peg board from the hardware store.

* Magnetic strips from the hardware store or sewing store can hold metal scissors or other metal tools.

* An empty can makes a great holder for tools, pencils, and paint brushes. You can decorate the can. Watch out for sharp edges! Wrap it in decorative paper and ribbon.

Always be safe when you are making something. Protect your eyes with safety glasses.

An engineer is always careful!

Don't forget these!

Metric System

Engineers use the metric system of measurement, so that is what Rosie uses here. But we've included standard measurements throughout too.

What special things will you add to your Engineer's Treasure?

_____
_____
_____
_____
_____
_____
_____
_____
_____
_____
_____
_____
_____
_____
_____
_____
_____
_____
_____
_____
_____
_____
_____

ASK: QUESTIONS! QUESTIONS! QUESTIONS!

Questions are tricky, and some hold on tight.
Questions kept Rosie awake through the night.

Think about all the questions you have and problems you'd like to solve. Write them here.

ENGINEERING STARTS WITH A QUESTION.

WHAT KIND OF ENGINEER?

Rosie likes to build machines and other inventions. Engineers who do that are called *mechanical engineers*. There are many, many different kinds of engineers!

There are many kinds of engineers.
Some work with chemicals; others with gears,
electrons or elements, liquids or light.
They help solve the problems of farming and flight.
In medicine, travel, safety, and sound,
an engineer's work can always be found.

They try to solve problems to help you live better,
from the water you drink to the threads in your sweater.
From your house, which stays warm on a cold winter day,
to the bus that you ride and the games that you play.

If a problem needs solving, the answer is clear:
Start with the help of a great engineer!

KINDS OF ENGINEERS

There are four main branches of engineering:

CIVIL, MECHANICAL, ELECTRICAL, CHEMICAL.

CIVIL engineers specialize in designing and building roads, bridges, buildings, and water-supply systems. There are many kinds of civil engineers.

- Environmental engineers manage pollution control, hazardous chemicals, global-warming issues, and waste.

- Structural engineers design the materials used in the construction of a building or other structure to make sure the frame is strong.

- Transportation engineers design roads, docks, sea terminals, and railroad tracks.

- River engineers study and change the course of rivers, if needed, for safety.

MECHANICAL engineers study motion, energy, and forces. They imagine, create, and manufacture all the mechanical objects in the world. That's a lot of objects! There are many kinds of mechanical engineers.

- Aerospace engineers create aircraft and spacecraft.

- Acoustical engineers improve the sound in speakers, hearing aids, and auditoriums.

- Automotive engineers research, design, and produce all the parts of a car and car safety.

- Manufacturing engineers figure out the best ways to turn products from raw materials to the packages on the shelf. (And the shelf itself!)

- Thermal engineers design and improve entire systems that control and regulate the transfer of thermal energy.

ELECTRICAL engineers design, develop, test, and supervise the manufacturing of electrical equipment. Here are some electrical engineers.

- Computer engineers imagine, design, and develop computers and the programs that run on them.

- Electronics engineers create microchips, circuits, and integrated circuits.

- Optical engineers use understanding of light and physics to create everything from CDs to lasers to huge telescopes.

- Power engineers convert energy sources into power (electricity).

CHEMICAL engineers work with atoms and molecules to create new chemicals or to change the properties of existing chemicals. They make new materials and fuels. Here are two:

- Materials engineers create and strengthen different materials used for making things.

- Petroleum engineers are involved in research, development, and production of fuels.

And then there are many, many kinds of engineers who <u>combine</u> these kinds of engineering.

There are so many more types of engineering that you can learn about at the library. Or you can ask an engineer!

WORD SEARCH

Can you find all the words listed to the right in the puzzle below?

(In case you need help, the answer key can be found on page 94.)

```
B T R A N S P O R T A T I O N J
I G F S G I N D U S T R I A L E
O A E A U T O M O T I V E S M E
M P R T R M A N U F A C T U R I
E O K C I T O P T I C A L Q I W
D W Q E H O M L E E N V I R O N
I E M L A I A H S T R U C T U R
C R U E W K T N I E R W A Y E V
A W P C E J K E M N A O Z A C O
L M Z T P R V S C I O U L G Y D
Y T C R R K D K S T N C H E M I
L P B O Y I O R Z R U I K O U D
Q Q V N N U C L E A R R N Q A M
V E I I Q M R A I B Y B A G M A
A A U C X G G R E M U M D L M Y
Y U B S P J V E L E C T R I C A
```

ACOUSTICAL COMPUTER   MECHANICAL   PETROLEUM
AEROSPACE   ELECTRICAL   MECHATRONIC   RIVER
AGRICULTURAL ELECTRONICS   METALLURGICAL SOFTWARE
ARCHITECTURAL ENVIRONMENTAL MINING   STRUCTURAL
AUTOMOTIVE INDUSTRIAL   NANOENGINEERS SYSTEMS
BIOMEDICAL MANUFACTURING NUCLEAR   THERMAL
CHEMICAL   MARINE   OPTICAL   ~~TRANSPORTATION~~
CIVIL   MATERIALS   POWER

```
Z  R  C  T  T  S  Y  S  T  E  M  S  R  I  N  B
S  A  G  R  I  C  U  L  T  U  R  A  L  S  U  L
H  A  T  R  O  N  I  C  A  K  T  T  O  L  A  V
G  J  L  M  C  N  S  S  K  O  K  E  A  C  S  E
Y  A  F  Q  H  K  M  I  Q  M  K  C  I  R  R  I
E  N  T  A  L  V  M  G  Q  U  I  G  E  A  U  U
L  C  O  M  P  U  T  E  R  N  R  E  W  P  X  Q
M  O  F  U  U  H  N  H  A  U  N  T  P  U  O  L
S  T  I  C  A  L  N  H  L  I  F  V  X  K  F  H
M  C  J  I  P  P  C  L  G  O  L  S  Y  R  T  V
A  L  I  V  D  E  A  N  S  T  H  E  R  M  A  L
J  U  P  I  M  T  E  J  M  X  R  V  U  J  O  K
K  W  E  L  E  O  C  S  K  M  Q  E  R  B  G  T
I  N  E  M  N  E  A  E  R  O  S  P  A  C  E  S
B  F  N  A  R  I  V  E  R  F  L  V  S  N  Y  Z
R  I  N  U  M  A  T  E  R  I  A  L  S  D  A  N
```

SIMPLE MACHINES!

Simple machines make the work of moving objects from one place to another easier. All the complicated machines we use are made of simple machines working together.

A **WHEEL** with an axle (a rod sticking through the wheel) moves an object easily.

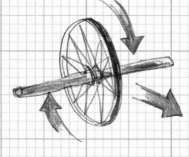

A **LEVER** is a stick that lets you lift an object.

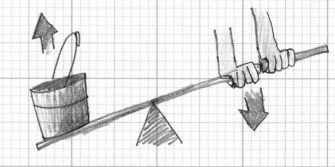

An **INCLINED PLANE** is a ramp that lets you move an object to a different level with less effort than lifting it.

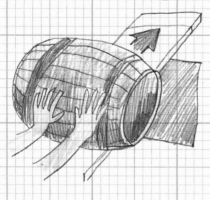

A **WEDGE** has at least one side that tapers into a sharp edge. A wedge cuts materials apart.

A **SCREW** is a wedge with an inclined plane wrapped around it.

A **PULLEY** is a rope over a wheel that allows you to lift heavy loads easily.

LOOK AROUND. Can you find these simple machines in your world? Some might be very big. Some might be very small. Draw them here:

An axle starts as just a stick
that's short or long, or thin or thick.
An axle, then, is no big deal—
until you put it with a wheel!

FANTASTIC FAILURES!

Engineers are great at solving problems because they know how to fail!

That sounds weird, but it's true. Engineers celebrate failure.
They learn from their mistakes and try again.

It was hard for Rosie to learn that lesson. When her heli-o-cheese-copter crashed, she was very upset and wanted to quit, but Great-Great-Aunt Rose helped her understand that failing is just part of learning! Great-Great-Aunt Rose is a mentor, or someone who helps someone else learn.

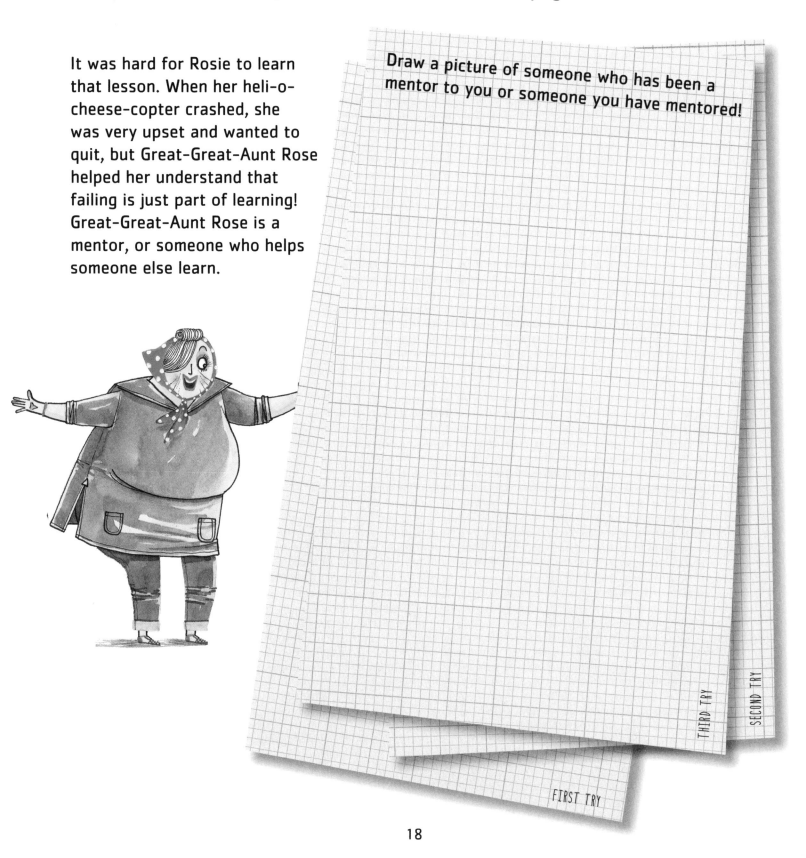

Draw a picture of someone who has been a mentor to you or someone you have mentored!

THIRD TRY

SECOND TRY

FIRST TRY

18

REINVENTING THE WHEEL!

Rosie's favorite invention is the bicycle. Here's how she improved it.

What's your favorite invention? Can you redesign it to make it even better?

MAKE IT!

Let's build a **SIMPLE CATAPULT**.
A catapult is a machine that hurls an object farther than you can throw it.
This is the simplest kind of catapult. It uses the force of your finger
to hurl a marshmallow or other small object.

MATERIALS

- 1 m (approximately 3') of narrow ribbon
- 1 rubber band
- 1 empty spool
- 1 plastic spoon
- 1 miniature marshmallow

Use the rubber band to fasten the ribbon to the center of the spool, with 8–10 cm (3–4") of ribbon extending beyond the spool.

Wrap the long end of the ribbon around the spool two or three times, covering the rubber band.

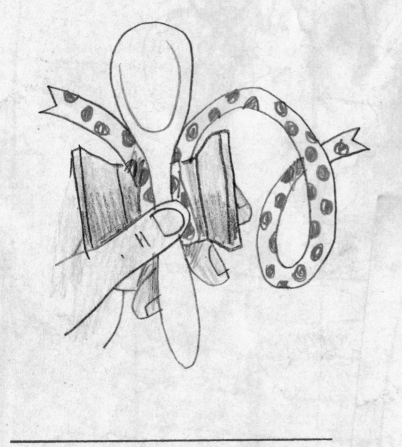

Place the spoon over the wrapped ribbon and hold it in place with your thumb.

Pull the ribbon across the spoon from lower right to upper left. Then pull the ribbon behind the spool and to the front again, keeping to the left of the spoon.

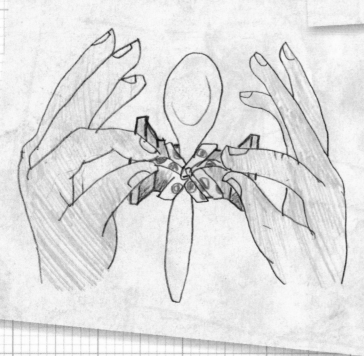

Cross the ribbon over the front of the spoon from bottom left to upper right, then circle the spool with the ribbon and bring it to the front, keeping to the right of the spoon handle.

Keep crisscrossing the ribbon over the spoon by pulling the ribbon over alternating sides of the spoon handle.

Don't worry if it's not perfect. It needs only to secure the spoon to the spool.

When the spoon is secure, tie the ends of the ribbon together.

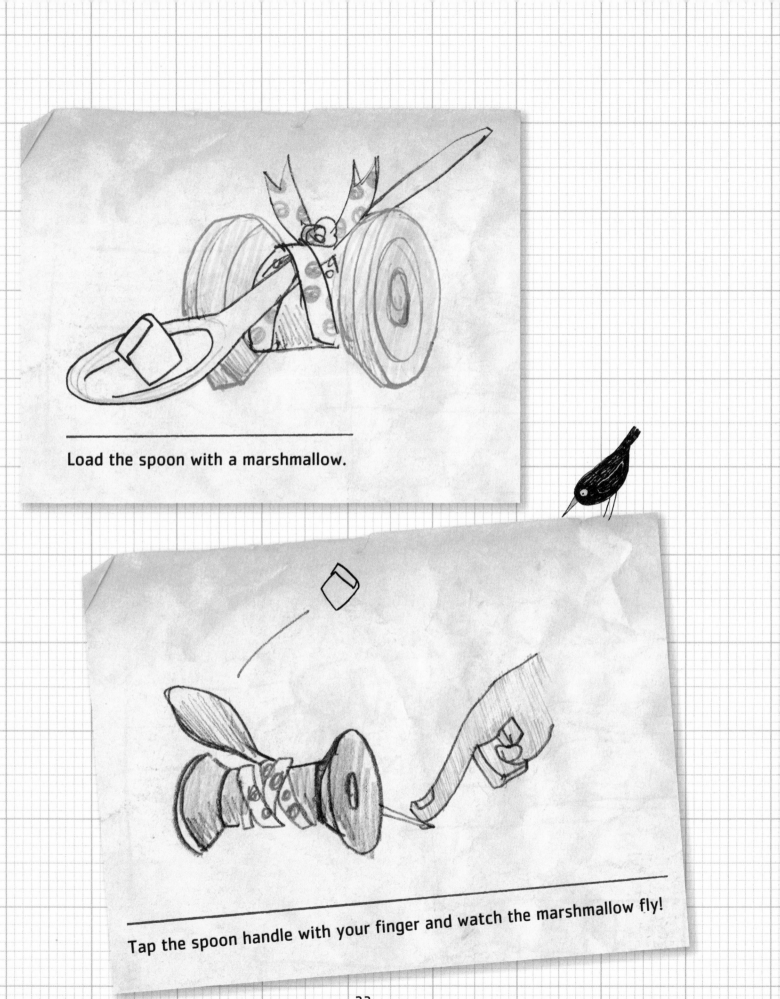

Load the spoon with a marshmallow.

Tap the spoon handle with your finger and watch the marshmallow fly!

CATAPULT ANALYSIS

How far does the marshmallow fly?

Can you improve the design?

What else can you toss with your catapult?
How far does it go?

GET BORED!

It's time to get bored out of your gourd.
Sit somewhere boring and do nothing.
Or at least try to do nothing. Can you do it?

Your brain never stops working. If you give it time and room to get bored, it will start thinking up ideas. Lots of ideas. Possibly brilliant ideas for things to invent!

WRITE YOUR INVENTION IDEAS HERE:

REAL-WORLD PROBLEMS

Having light in your house lets you read books and study at night.
You might be reading at night right now!

Millions of kids around the world do not have access to artificial light. Without lights, they can't study at night, and night might be the only time they don't have chores to do. This makes it difficult to get a good education.

Engineers are working on batteries that are charged by solar energy or by motion, which is called *kinetic energy*. These batteries power small lights that families can use to light their homes at night. One design is a soccer ball that stores energy each time it is kicked. Another collects energy from a yo-yo!

Think about all the ways you move in a day. Design a device that collects your motion to power a light.

Kinetic to electric . . .

The transfer of kinetic energy to electricity can be done in many ways. For now, don't worry about that step.

While brainstorming your design, include a red diamond to represent the transfer mechanism.

SUPER-DUPER ENGINEERING CHALLENGE

Sometimes engineers design new things,
but often what they do is improve existing things.

Great-Great-Aunt Rose walks with a cane. She also loves
to make things and fix things. Can you adapt her cane to
carry some of her tools?

Draw your adaptations on her cane on the next page
and use the pieces of "paper" to take notes on
what each adaptation is for.

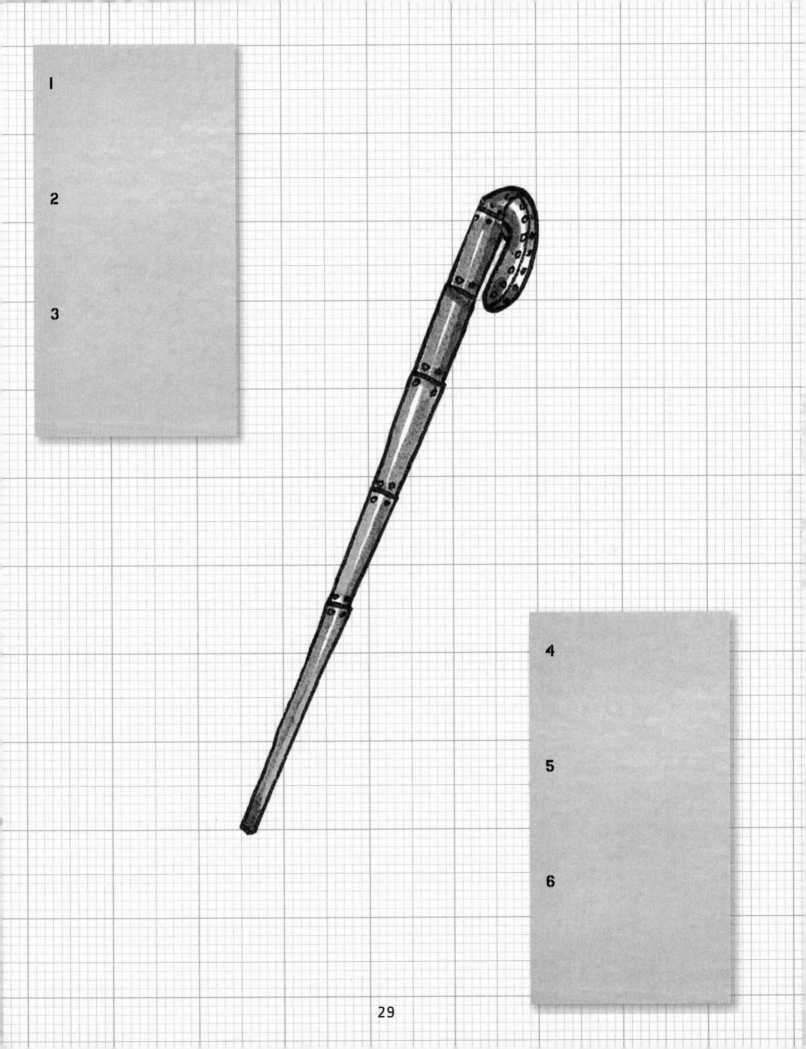

ENGINEERING DESIGN PROCESS

It takes a long time, hard work, and many tries to solve problems. Engineers follow a set of steps called the *engineering design process.* It helps them figure out what to do next. Here is a simple version to follow.

ASK: What questions do you want to answer? What problem do you want to solve?

IMAGINE: Explore ideas that could lead you to an answer to your question or an invention to solve the problem. This process is also called *brainstorming!*

PLAN: Figure out how to make your invention. This is called a *design.* What will you need? What steps will you take? Make lists and instructions to follow.

CREATE: Follow your plan and make that invention! You might have to change your design as you go along. That's okay! Keep notes about things you learn as you go.

IMPROVE: Evaluate your invention. Did it work as you expected? What went right? What went wrong? Follow your observations to figure out what problems you want to solve and questions you want to answer next! That's how you get back to the beginning!

REMEMBER: Engineering is not a thing. It's a process. And that's why it's fun!

BUILD IT! TEST IT! EVALUATE IT!

Build your invention and give it a test!

Evaluation is what comes next.

How did it work? Did it do what you thought?

Sometimes that happens. But more often not.

A fantastic failure? A fabulous flop?

It's time to get busy. There's no time to stop!

"Life might have its failures, but this is not it!

The only true failure can come if you quit!"

31

IMAGINE: BRAINSTORMING TIME!

When you think up new ideas to solve a problem, you're brainstorming.
You can use the same steps here as in your design process:
ASK, IMAGINE, PLAN, CREATE, IMPROVE.

EVERY idea is a good one when brainstorming. Even the weird, silly, and goofy ones! Sometimes those are the ideas that take you to the solution!

Use these pages to brainstorm a solution to a problem
or an answer to a question.

Brainstorm! Brainstorm! Brainstorm!

Like a rainstorm
stuck inside your head.

Except that it's not made of rain
but great big thoughts instead.

PLAN: DESIGN TIME!

After you brainstorm ideas to solve a problem, pick a solution you'd like to explore further.

Ask yourself questions. Think about how the solution might work and the materials you might need to build your machine, and plan how you might make it. This is called *design*.

Use these pages to explore your idea and create a design.

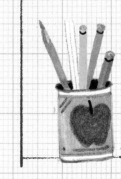

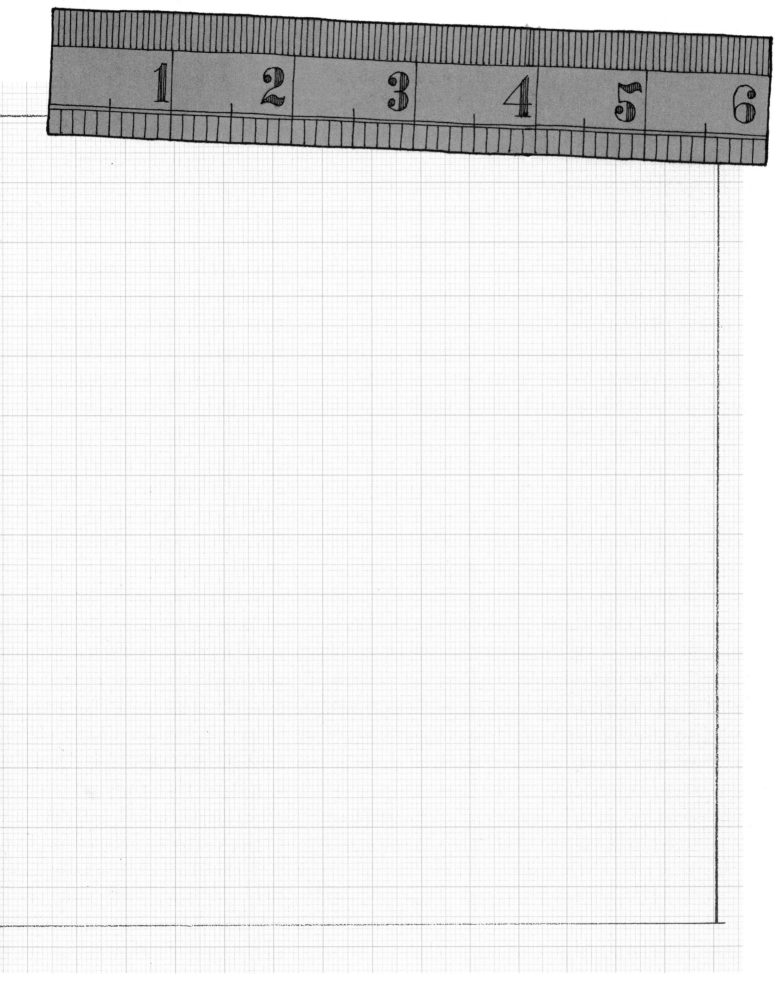

CELEBRATE YOUR FABULOUS FLOPS!

Think about a time you failed at something and wanted to quit.
Draw a picture to show how you felt. What did you learn?

Every failure is a step forward, if you learn from it!

CELEBRATE YOUR SUPER SUCCESSES!

Draw a picture of something you've done or created that made you proud.

SUPER-DUPER ENGINEERING CHALLENGE

Rosie is helping Uncle Fred at the zoo. You can help, too! This is your chance to brainstorm, design, and build an invention to help Rosie and Uncle Fred!

You can use any materials you wish. There is no wrong answer to this challenge, just lots of chances to make fabulous failures—and to learn!

The orangutans are clever primates. They taught themselves to use branches as levers and pried open the gate to their enclosure. After that, they taught the other primates to use levers, too. One night, they opened all the enclosures and let the zoo animals roam free. Then they played catch with all the eggs they could find in the zoo. That's a lot of eggs.

When Uncle Fred arrived at the zoo, it was pandemonium!

It took the zookeepers all day to get the animals back into the right enclosures. And another day for Uncle Fred to locate all the missing eggs. He doesn't want to touch them and risk his scent confusing the animals, so he needs an invention that can gather the eggs and put them into a container.

The orangutans were very clever—
Taught themselves to use a lever.
Opened doors and cages, too.
Now it's chaos at the zoo!

Rosie wants to build the Eggster-1000 Egg Picker-Upper.
Can you help her design it?

Now, use your Engineer's Treasure to build your design!

REDESIGNING THE WHEEL!

Design a stuffed-animal carrier for your bike that keeps your stuffed animals dry if you hit a puddle but also lets them have a view of the road ahead.

DRAW YOUR DESIGN HERE:

REAL-WORLD PROBLEMS

Many families around the world live in areas without enough fuel for cooking. The fuel that is available is often highly pollutive, causes health problems, and contributes to climate change. Can you design a way to use the energy of the sun or wind to cook food?

SUPER-DUPER ENGINEERING CHALLENGE

Are you ready for another challenge?

This is a platypus. Its egg is smaller than a lima bean.

This is an echidna (ee-KID-na). Its egg is small and leathery.

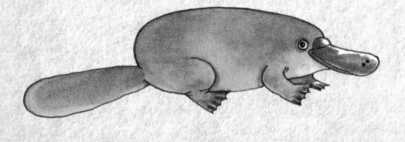

1. ___

2. ___

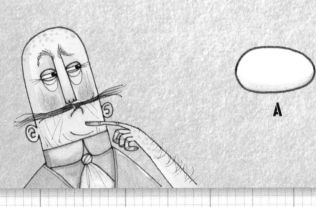

A

B

It took all day for Uncle Fred to pick up the eggs. Now he has to sort them and get them back to their parents.

How can Uncle Fred tell whose egg is whose?
Can you help Rosie and Uncle Fred sort the eggs at the zoo?

(*Hint*: Color, size, and texture can help him identify the eggs. Weight can help, too.)

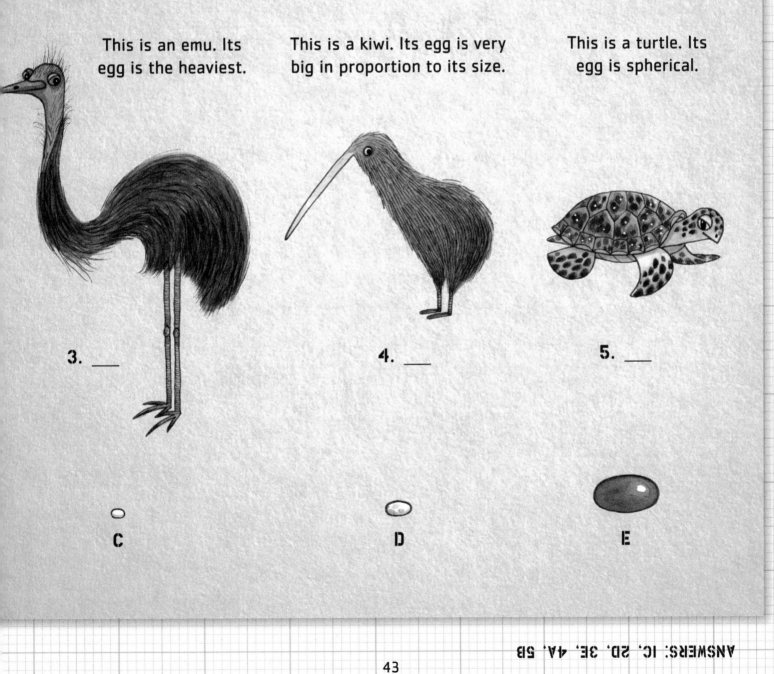

This is an emu. Its egg is the heaviest.

This is a kiwi. Its egg is very big in proportion to its size.

This is a turtle. Its egg is spherical.

3. ___

4. ___

5. ___

C

D

E

Can you design a scale to weigh the eggs Uncle Fred has collected?

- Use a spoon to load the eggs onto the scale.
- Use pennies as the unit of weight.

You can sketch here and then build your invention with items in your Engineer's Treasure.

SUPER SQUIRREL CHALLENGE

Birds love birdseed. But guess who else loves it? Squirrels!

Squirrels are clever and determined. If they want birdseed,
they will do anything to get it.

Can you design a birdfeeder that lets the birds get the seeds
while keeping out the squirrels?

MYSTERY MACHINE!

Can you design a machine that turns these thingies into the delicious "gizmo" at the bottom of the page? Draw your mystery machine inside the box.

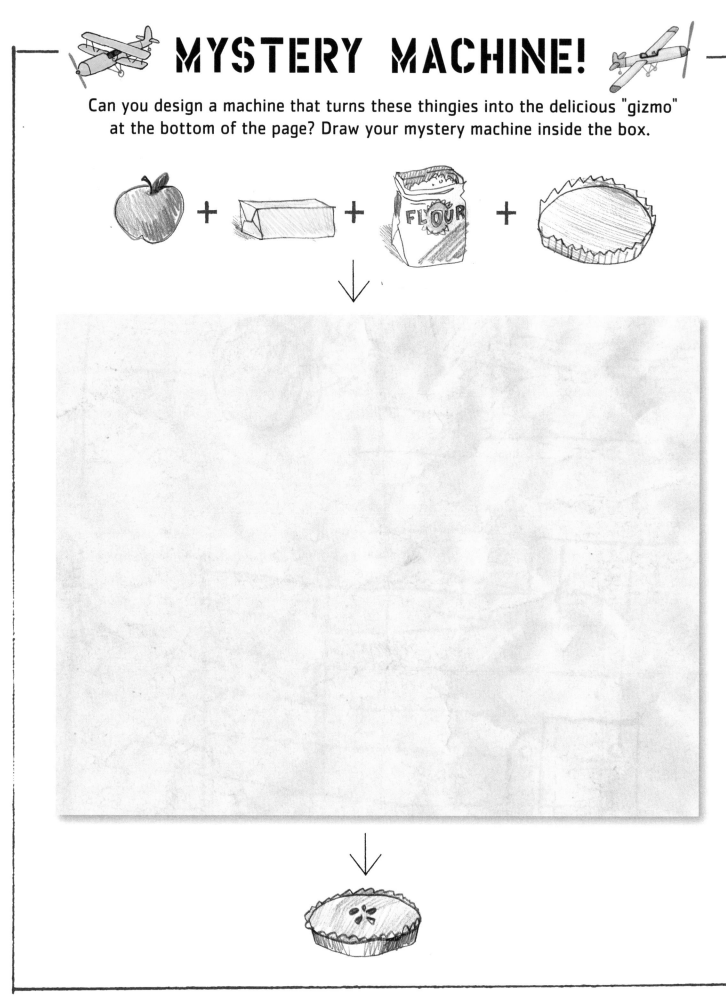

ENGINEERS ARE HELPFUL!

Rosie is kind and helps her uncles and aunts.

Can you think of a time when you helped someone? What did you do?

DRAW A PICTURE TO SHOW IT.

JUST DOODLE!

Creativity is essential for engineers. It lets them look at problems in new ways.
Drawing is a great way to exercise your imagination.

DRAW A PICTURE OF AN IMAGINARY PLACE YOU'D LIKE TO VISIT.

REAL-WORLD PROBLEMS

Sometimes, gripping a door handle can be difficult. You have your hands full or, like some people, you might have a medical condition that makes it painful to grip things.

Design a gizmo to help you open doors with your elbows.

ARE YOU A QUITTER?

Rosie and Great-Great-Aunt Rose failed again and again when they built the heli-o-cheese-copter. But each time, they got closer to success. Inventors have to be persistent and not give up.

SWAN . . . AND HARRY

Most people think that Thomas Edison invented the first lightbulb, but that's not true. The first electric lightbulb was created by English inventor Sir Joseph Wilson Swan in 1860. He was an inventor with a long name and an even longer beard. His beard was so long it had a name of its own. It was called Harry. Actually, that part isn't true.

What is true is that Swan worked for many years to improve his lightbulb. In 1878, he gave the word's first lightbulb demonstration. Wowza! However, his bulb would not burn for very long, and it was not practical for commercial use or for use in homes.

Thomas Edison created a version of the lightbulb that could burn for more than 600 hours (later bulbs burned much, much longer). He and his team of engineers tested carbonized filaments from plants around the world to find the one that would burn the longest. It was the bamboo fiber! (Lightbulbs use tungsten fibers now.)

Some reports say that Edison tested a thousand filaments to find the best choice. Others say six thousand. Some even say ten thousand! Can you imagine trying something over and over so many times? That takes persistence!

EDISON

How persistent are you? Can you draw a thousand lightbulbs in the space below? (Use some scrap paper if you need more space.)

Thomas Edison had a team of assistants who helped him. He called them the "Muckers" because they "mucked about" in the lab with him.

If you want, you can also get a team of Muckers to help with your lightbulbs!

FANTASTIC FLOPS!

Swan and Edison failed over and over and over.
What if they had given up and never finished the lightbulb?
Can you imagine your house or your school with no lightbulbs?
How would that change your life?

DRAW HERE:

PATENT, PLEASE!

Rosie makes gizmos and gadgets and doohickeys, too.
She also gives them great names like the "heli-o-cheese-copter."

Make a list of awesome invention names.

Go back through the book and give fanciful, descriptive names to your terrific inventions.

MAKE IT!

Here's a design for a basic **SOLAR OVEN**.
This is a simple design that can be used on warm, sunny days.
Build it and test it . . . and then see if you can improve it!

MATERIALS

Standard poster board (22" x 28")

1 can of flat black paint

1 paintbrush

1 old metal pie pan

Glue stick or bottle of glue and brush

1 roll of aluminum foil

1 roll of clear packing tape

1 pair of scissors

1 Sharpie marker

Clean, small or medium poultry roasting bags, with twist ties

2 or 3 small wooden blocks

1 tube of your favorite cookie dough

Paint the bottom (NOT the inside) of metal pie plate with flat black paint. Allow to dry.

Clear a workspace large enough to allow the poster board to lie flat.

Remove the roll of foil from the box.

Starting at bottom right corner of your poster, apply a 10 x 10 cm (4" x 4") patch of glue along the edge.

Note: The goal is to create a large, flat, shiny surface. Try to make the surface as smooth as possible, but don't worry if there are creases or crinkles. Your solar oven will still work.

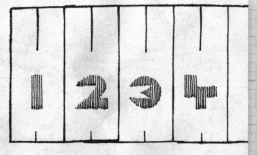

54

Position the roll of foil (with the shiny side up) on the glue, allowing 5 cm (2") of foil to hang over top edge and side edge of poster.

Gently unroll the foil to cover the exposed glue.

Smooth the glued section of foil by pressing down gently but firmly with your hand.

Apply glue over next 10 x 10 cm (4" x 4") section of poster.

Continue painting glue onto the poster board and rolling the foil over the glue until you reach the end of the poster board.

Using the scissors, cut the roll of foil 5 cm (2") past the edge of the poster board.

Smooth down the foil. Take care not to get glue on the shiny side of the poster board.

Repeat process on the remaining sections, being sure to leave 5 cm (2") of foil to hang over the edge on all sides, until the poster board is completely covered in foil. Smooth gently.

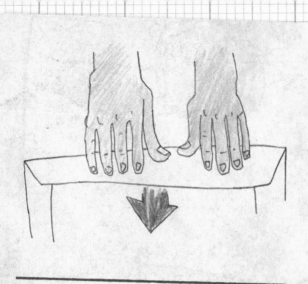

Flip the poster board over. Working in sections, fold over and glue down the visible foil and press to smooth.

Flip the poster board again so the shiny side is up.

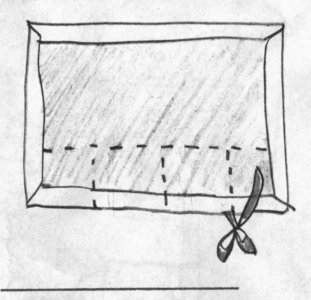

Using a ruler and a marker, draw several dots to mark 18 cm (7") from the bottom of the poster board. Use these dots to draw a line across the poster board, lengthwise.

Fold the shiny side together at the line.
Unfold.

Cut three straight lines from the bottom of the poster board to the fold, as shown.

Cuts should be at 18 cm, 36 cm, and 54 cm (7", 14", and 21") from the left edge of the poster board.

Stand the poster board up, so that it rests on the newly cut flaps.

Pull flaps 1 and 4 together until they touch.

Tape the bottom of all flaps in position using clear packing tape.

This is your solar oven.

*** Always wear sunglasses when working with reflective materials in the sun. The sun's rays are powerful and can harm your eyes!

*** Ask for adult supervision and use baking mitts to handle the hot pan.

LET'S COOK!

- On a warm, sunny day, open the cookie dough and press it into the pie pan. Place the pan in the poultry bag that is closest in size and seal the bag. The goal is to heat the air surrounding the pie pan to help cook the dough. However, if the bag is too big, too much energy will be used heating the air and not the dough!

- Place block(s) as needed to support the pie pan in the bag. This allows the heated air to circulate around the bottom of the pie pan and bake the cookie evenly.

- Best time to cook: It is best to cook when your shadow is the shortest (when the sun is closest to its high point in the sky).

- Place your solar oven in the sun and position it so that it catches the most rays possible. The foil reflects the sun's rays down toward your cookie bag, where they collect, heating up the air inside the bag. The black paint on the bottom of your pie pan absorbs the heat and helps cook the dough.

- Leave in the sun to bake. Occasionally, rotate the solar oven to track the sun's rays.

Depending on the time of year, the temperature, and the position of the sun, cooking time can vary from 1 hour to 3 hours. You will know the cookie is done when the dough is brown and crispy at the edges.

EAT THAT COOKIE!

MYSTERY MACHINE!

Can you design a machine that turns these thingies into a gizmo?
Draw the machine *and* the gizmo this time.

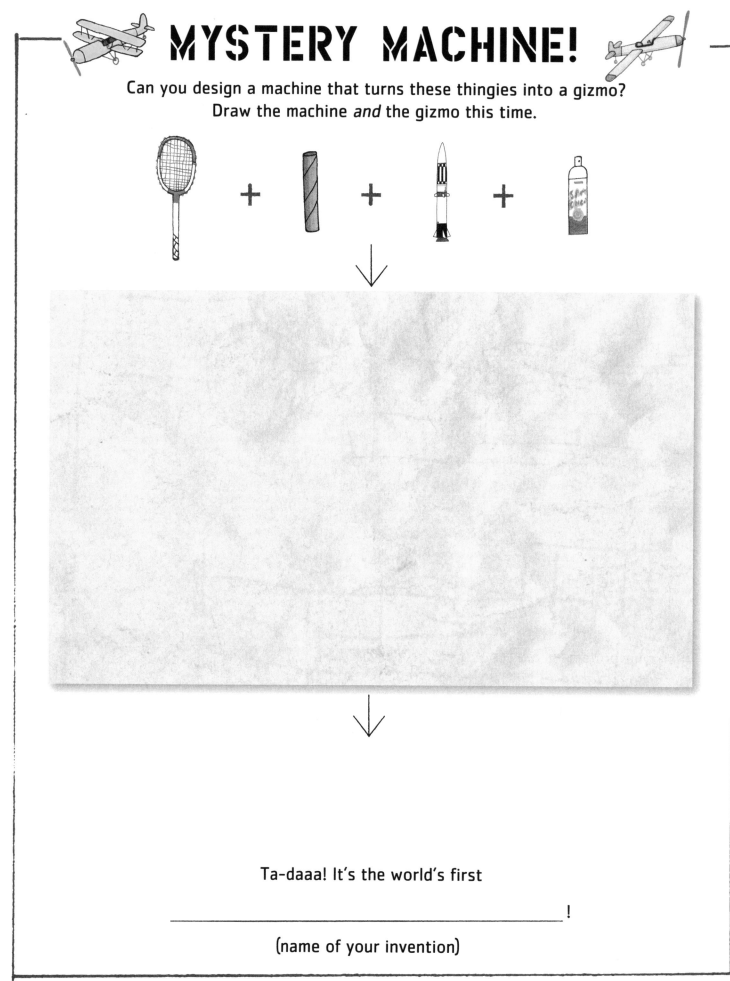

Ta-daaa! It's the world's first

_____!

(name of your invention)

TRAITS OF GREAT ENGINEERS

Working in teams is important for engineers. Team members share ideas and ask questions to improve designs. They challenge one another to think about problems in new ways. Team members with different backgrounds can offer new points of view, which can lead to unexpected solutions!

Circle traits that would be helpful for you and your team members to have.
Are there other traits you would add?

Smart	Good at listening	Clever	Bald	_____
Creative	Itchy	Funny	Loves math	_____
Observant	Friendly	Likes to travel	Loves art	_____
Green	Bold	Knows how to sew	Loves science	_____
Organized	Good at drawing	Understands biology	Loves tacos	_____

RULES FOR WORKING AS A TEAM

Working as a team is fun, but it can also be a challenge. Some basic rules help teams work smoothly.

- Listen and ask questions.

- Respect other people's opinions, talents, and time!

- Be open to new points of view. There are many ways to solve most problems. Your solution might not be the best way. If others disagree with your ideas, it does not mean that they reject you!

- Brainstorming is about collecting all ideas—even the weird ones. When brainstorming, never say "No!" to an idea. Instead, say, "Let's think about it." Then think about it! Sometimes the weirdest ideas help you find the best answer.

- Be flexible. Give other people's ideas a chance.

- Don't be a time hog. Let others take turns.

Working as a team doesn't mean that you will all agree completely on a solution. That's okay. Go with the idea that most people can support. Give it a try. Then see how it can be improved. That's the engineering way!

Draw a picture of your engineering team. It can have people you know and also people you imagine.

SUPER-DUPER ENGINEERING CHALLENGE

The Snooty Agouti and the Nut-Chucker

In the far back corner of Blue River Creek Zoo, there is an enclosure surrounded by a box hedge with dark, waxy leaves. There lives an agouti. Her name is Trudy.

Trudy the Agouti looks like this:

Like all agoutis, she has a plump rump and a very stout snout, which helps her smell very well. Trudy the Agouti came from the forests of Costa Rica, and she loves nuts and berries. What Trudy the Agouti does not love is people. She turns up her nose at the slightest whiff of them.

This is a problem for Uncle Fred. He can't touch her food, and if he enters the enclosure to feed Trudy, she hides and won't eat the nuts or berries he leaves for her.

Uncle Fred loves Trudy the Agouti and wants her to eat well. He has tried many ways to deliver her food, but nothing has worked. Once, he even disguised himself as an agouti, but Trudy was not fooled. His mustache gave him away.

The answer? A nut-chucker.

Uncle Fred needs a nut-chucker to lob nuts over the hedge. Can you design one?

Here are some details:

- The nut-chucker must be able to lob a nut over the hedge, which is 30 cm (1') wide and 30 cm (1') tall. Test with a Ping-Pong ball.

- The nut-chucker must operate from the opposite side of the hedge from Trudy. It must also stay on the ground when chucking nuts so that Trudy does not see it.

- It must be at least 50 cm (approximately 18") from the closest edge of the hedge. The farther the better, so Trudy the Agouti doesn't get a whiff of the operator.

- No one can touch the nuts (or the Ping-Pong balls during testing). Use a spoon or other tool to load the nut-chucker.

Get busy! Trudy the Agouti is hungry!

REAL-WORLD PROBLEMS

The world is covered with water. Three-quarters of the world's surface is wet. Even so, we have a terrible water crisis on the planet. Imagine that the world is a big orange with a straw sticking into it and we are drinking all the juice! We stand on the thin crust of the earth and pull water from the gigantic water "tanks" deep in the Earth (called "aquifers"). Water returns to the aquifers through rain, which soaks into the ground. However, we are using water faster than the rain can put it back into the aquifers. We are sucking the planet dry!

Every bit of water we can save helps preserve the aquifers.

How can you help? Find ways to save water. Think about how you use water. Can you find ways to use less?

USE YOUR ENGINEERING SKILLS TO BRAINSTORM IDEAS!

CRAZY MACHINES!

This is Rube Goldberg. He was a famous cartoonist who drew more than 50,000 cartoons in his lifetime. He is most famous for cartoons of zany machines that do simple tasks in the most complicated ways possible. Goldberg was an expert at imagining inventions because—guess what?—he was an engineer.

A Rube Goldberg machine is a very complicated machine that performs a very simple task. One of his inventions puts a hole in a doughnut. The machine involves a hammer, a coconut, a board, a cat, a film projector, a diver, and a diving board. See more of Rube Goldberg's machines at www.rubegoldberg.com

Can you draw your own Rube Goldberg machine to pick up tiny building blocks from your floor?

ENGINEERS ARE OBSERVANT!

Engineers pay attention to what goes on around them. Watch your family.
What do they do every day? Are there things that are difficult for them to do?
Can you think of ways to help?

BRAINSTORM IDEAS HERE:

BIG "WHAT IF?" QUESTIONS

Sometimes engineers tackle practical, real-world problems.
Sometimes they ask great big "What if?" questions. For instance . . .

WHAT IF YOU LIVED ON THE MOON?

Moon facts:

- The Moon was formed 4.6 billion years ago. That's older than most knock-knock jokes but younger than the Earth by about 40 million years.

- The Moon's average distance from Earth is approximately 385,000 kilometers (240,000 miles or so), but it is moving a little farther away each year. Was it something we said?

- The Moon orbits Earth every 27.3 Earth days.

- The Moon has weaker gravity than Earth. On the Moon, you would weigh about one-sixth of your weight on Earth.

- There is no atmosphere on the Moon to protect its surface from cosmic rays, meteorites, or solar winds. It can also be very cold: colder than minus 150 degrees Celsius (minus 300 degrees Fahrenheit). And very hot: hotter than plus 120 degrees Celsius (plus 200 degrees Fahrenheit). There is no sound because there are no gas molecules to transfer the sound waves, as on Earth.

Atmospheres are fantastic. Our atmosphere wraps around Earth like a blanket made of gases. It keeps Earth's temperatures in a range that we can tolerate and it protects us from all the deadly things that hit the surface of the Moon. Taking care of our atmosphere is vital. That's why we must limit pollution that harms the atmosphere.

If you lived on the Moon, you'd need all the things you need on Earth: air, water, food, and a safe place to live. And games to play.

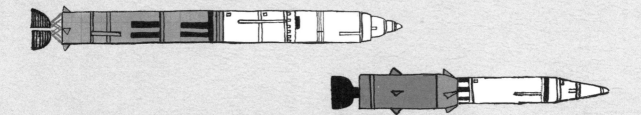

DRAW YOUR DESIGNS FOR LIFE ON THE MOON!

MAKE IT!

Here's a plan for a **MARBLE RUN**.
Use extra paper towel tubes to make your run as long as you like!

MATERIALS

1 empty toilet paper tube

1 roll of Scotch tape

1 screw

2 paper clips

2 empty paper towel tubes

2 equal lengths of narrow ribbon, approximately 60 cm (2') each

1 empty cereal box

1 pair of scissors

1 bamboo skewer

2 thread bobbins (best if containing some thread)

1 roll of painter's tape (easily removable and doesn't damage door or walls)

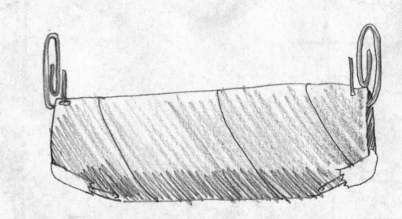

Pinch the ends of a toilet paper tube and tape in place, as shown.

Use the screw to make a hole at either end of the tube opposite the taped area. Attach the paper clips.

Tie the ribbons to the paper clips.

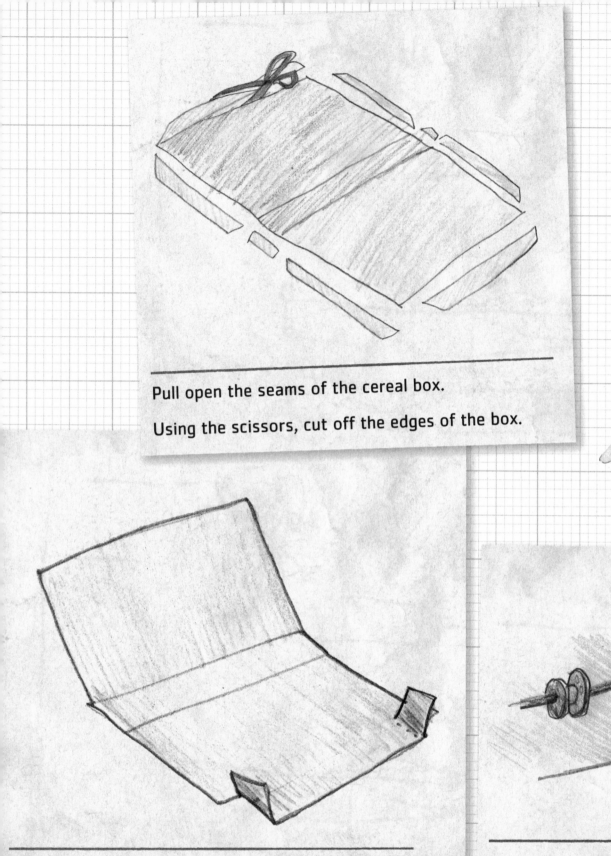

Pull open the seams of the cereal box.

Using the scissors, cut off the edges of the box.

Make a 6 cm (2.5") cut into the box 6 cm (2.5") from each end.

Fold as shown to create two flaps.

Twist the screw into the center of one flap to create a hole. Repeat on the other flap.

Push the bamboo skewer through the hole in one of the flaps.

73

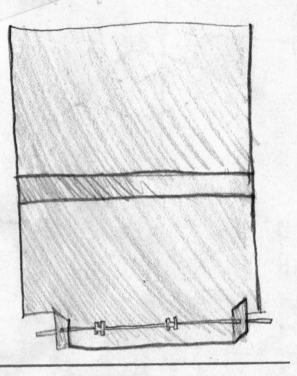

Push the bamboo skewer through the center of the two bobbins, then through the hole in the other the flap.

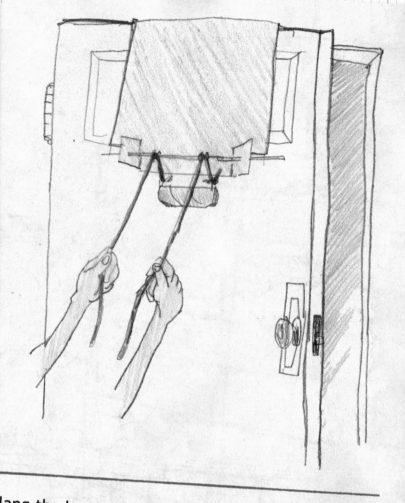

Hang the box over the top of a door.

Drape the toilet paper roll over the bobbins with the ribbons, as shown.

Practice controlling the tube by pulling on the ribbons together or separately.

Move the tube from side to side along the skewer.

Cut out a rectangle of cardboard from one end of a paper towel tube, large enough for a marble to fit through.

Tape the paper towel tubes together to form a marble run beneath the cereal box and in range of the toilet paper tube marble dispenser.

Use the painter's tape to tape the run to the door. You can also use the tape to stabilize the cereal box over the door.

Maneuver the smaller tube to drop marbles into the run.

Add more tubes to your run for a more elaborate marble course.

Have fun!

BIG "WHAT IF" QUESTIONS

WHAT IF YOU LIVED UNDER THE SEA?

To live under the sea, you'd need access to air, food, energy,
and protection from the many things that could harm you:
high pressure from water above you, strong currents, lava,
hot acid from vents in the crust, and, possibly, very cranky krakens.

Learn more about the ocean by reading the deep-sea facts, then design your
Deep Sea Dwelling.

DRAW IT HERE:

Deep-sea facts:

- 71 percent of Earth is covered by ocean.

- Oceans are deep and dark. They average approximately 730 m (approximately 2,400') in depth, but the sun's light reaches through only the top 100 m (300' or so).

- Humans have explored less than 5 percent of the ocean floor.

- There are mountain chains beneath the ocean and underwater pillars that are several stories high and spew sulfuric acid.

- The ocean is full of life—more than 50 percent of life on Earth lives below the surface of the ocean. Life exists even in the most hostile spots in the ocean. There are tubeworms 3 m long (approximately 10') that live in the hot springs under the ocean floor, where temperatures can reach 340 degrees Celsius (650 degrees Fahrenheit). That's hot enough to melt lead!

- If you are beneath the ocean, all the water above you weighs down on you. That's a lot of water. The pressure deep in the ocean is strong enough to crush the *Titanic*. Even so, animals live there!

- The ocean is very powerful but also very fragile.

   Every year, three times more trash goes into the ocean than there are fish taken out of the ocean.

   Fertilizer from farms and lawns dumps extra nutrients into the ocean. These cause enormous algae blooms, which deplete the water of dissolved oxygen. Without oxygen, the marine life suffocates. The result is enormous dead zones in the ocean.

   Climate change caused by our extensive use of fossil fuels adds to the rising temperatures of the ocean and makes the dead zones even deader.

ENGINEERS MAKE THINGS BETTER!

Most inventions change over time as engineers refine designs and make improvements to previous models.

Consider the bicycle! The bicycles you see today are very different from the bicycle that was invented in 1790.

Can you design a bicycle for the future? Will it be able to travel up walls? Over lakes? Through the air? On the Moon?

Will it play music? Water the yard? Keep away mosquitoes?

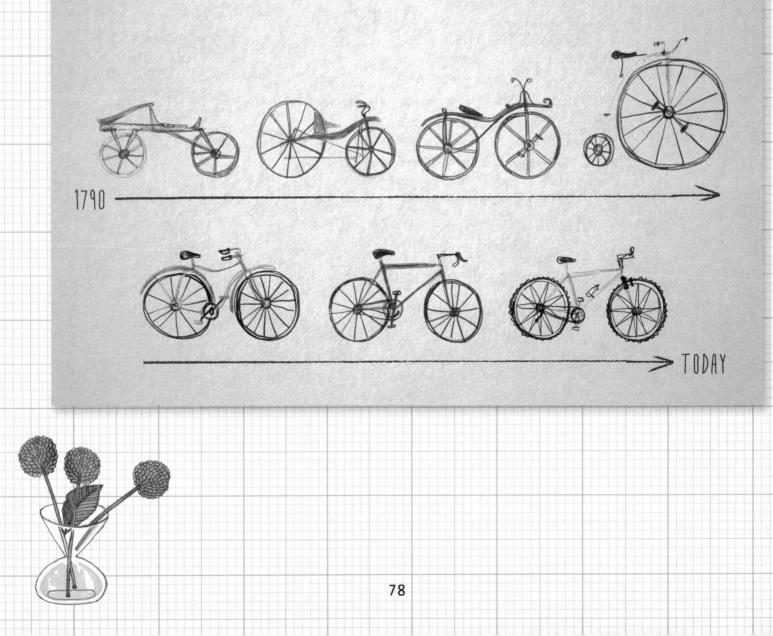

1790

TODAY

DRAW YOUR DESIGN HERE:

LOOK TO NATURE!

Nature is amazing! Engineers find lots of ideas
by observing animals and plants.

The inventor of Velcro observed the plant stickers that clung to his pants
when he walked through a field. The stickers held tightly—but were
also easy to remove. He used them as a model for the hook-and-loop
fasteners that make up Velcro.

Look around nature. What do you see? Write your questions and
observations here. Use them to brainstorm ideas for your new inventions!

Draw an animal that can do something humans can't. Can you design a
machine to do the same thing?

MACHINE

ANIMAL

MYSTERY MACHINE!

Can you design a machine that turns these thingies into a gizmo?
This time draw the thingies, machine, *and* gizmo!

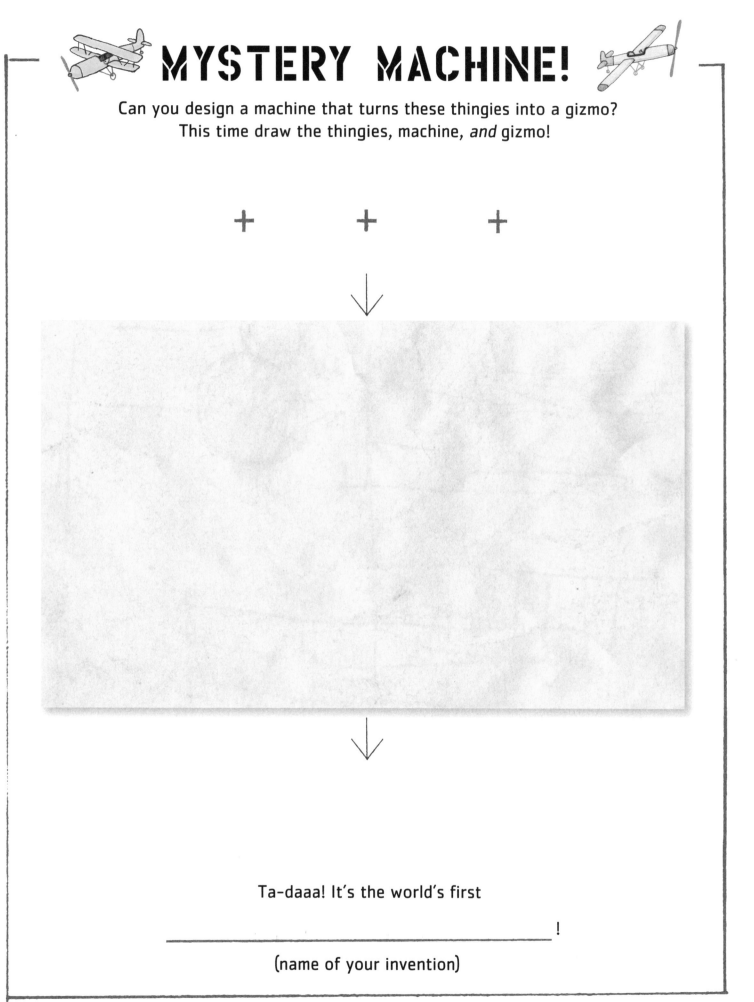

+   +   +

Ta-daaa! It's the world's first

_____!

(name of your invention)

DESIGN CHALLENGE!

Using your Engineer's Treasure (or Rosie's) for inspiration, design a game you can play with a friend. Use this space to design it and list the rules.

RULES:

MAKE IT!

Let's make a **SIMPLE CAR**.

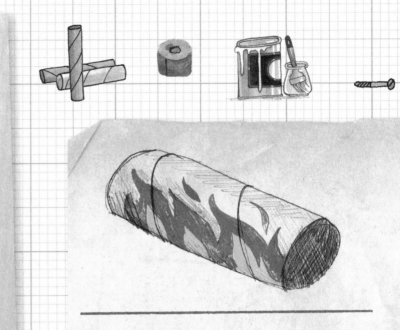

MATERIALS

1 empty paper towel tube

Paints and paintbrushes, markers, stickers

1 screw

1 bamboo skewer

4 recycled CDs or DVDs

1 roll of duct tape

1 jar of adhesive putty or modeling clay

Paint the tube as desired. Allow paint to dry.

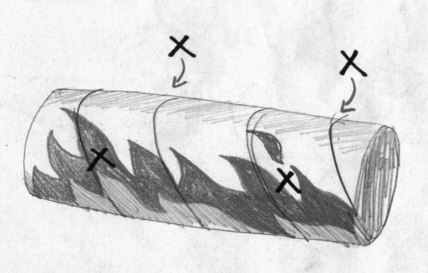

On one side of the tube, mark an X approximately 5 cm (2") from each end and at least 12 cm (5") apart.

Repeat on the opposite side, making sure the Xs are at the exact same height and distance from the end as those on the other side of the tube.

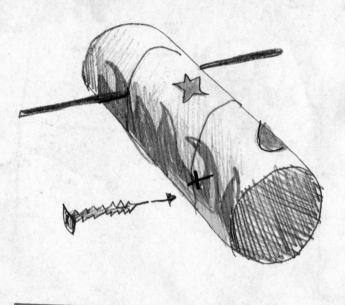

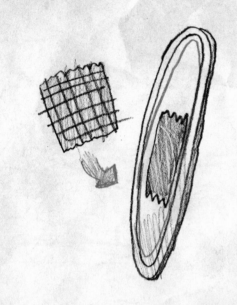

Use stickers and markers for additional decoration, taking care not to cover the Xs.

Firmly twist the screw into each X marked on the tube to form a hole. Unscrew to remove screw.

Cut the bamboo skewer in half.

Poke one of the bamboo skewers through the hole on one side of the tube and out the hole on the opposite side of the tube. Repeat for the other end of the tube. These are the car's axles.

Cut 5-cm (2") squares of duct tape and cover the holes in the CDs or DVDs on both sides.

Use the screw to form a small hole in the center of each piece of duct tape.

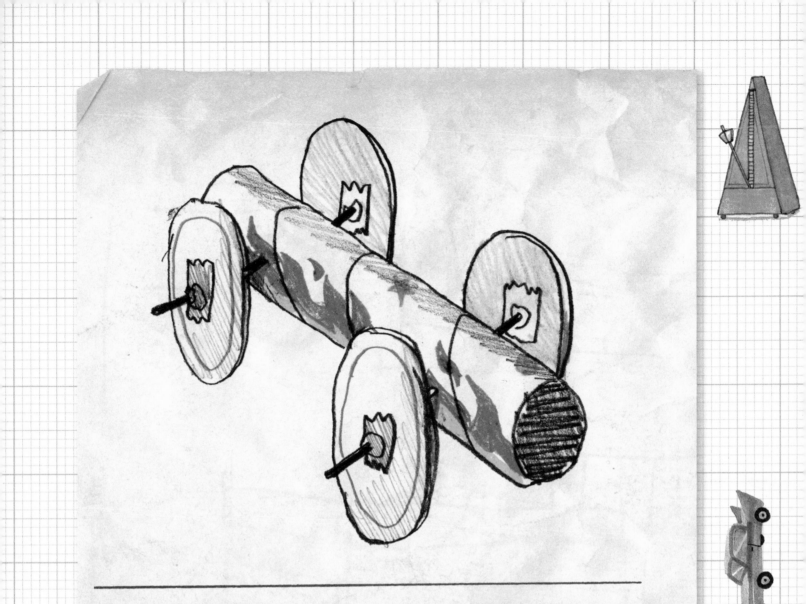

One by one, push the CDs or DVDs onto the skewers, one on each piece sticking out. (Confirm that no one is still *using* the DVDs or CDs first!)

Secure the "wheels" with additional tape (or adhesive putty or clay) on both sides of the CDs or DVDs at the skewer to provide stability, if needed.

The axles should move freely.

Each wheel should turn parallel to body of the tube and the other wheels.

Wheels that wobble or are not parallel will take energy away from the forward motion of your car.

Test your car. Push it gently on floor or roll it down a ramp or hill.

AUTOMOTIVE EXAMINATION

Did it go straight?

Did it go far?

Did the wheels wobble?

Can you improve the design using other supplies from your Engineer's Treasure to make the wheels work more efficiently?

Test your car again!

How did it do? Can you measure how far it went?

Can you improve your design and test it again?

That's the engineer's way!

SUPER-DUPER ENGINEERING CHALLENGE

Can you help Rosie design and make a hat for Uncle Fred?

There are lots of words to describe Uncle Fred: *affable, convivial, exuberant, ebullient, jocund, joyous,* and *jubilant.*

They all mean that Uncle Fred is full of joy and loves to laugh. A lot.

When Uncle Fred laughs, he really laughs. He chortles and chuckles and giggles and guffaws and hoots and howls and snorts and snickers. Sometimes he laughs so hard that his eyes fill with tears and he tilts to one side and almost falls over. This is fine, except on Thursdays.

On Thursdays, Uncle Fred tours the entire zoo. If he passes by the hyenas and they laugh—which they always do—Uncle Fred laughs, too. He laughs so hard that he runs out of time and energy to finish the tour.

Uncle Fred asked Rosie to make him a snack hat so he can get more energy and finish the tour even if he starts laughing with the hyenas.

Can you help design Uncle Fred's hat?

Create a snack dispenser that Uncle Fred can wear on his head.

Use items from your Engineer's Treasure plus an existing hat (or make a hat of your own).

REQUIREMENTS

- The dispenser must drop cheese cubes 1 cm x 1 cm (½" x ½") into Uncle Fred's hand.

- The dispenser must stay on Uncle Fred's head while he uses it.

- It should not spill if Uncle Fred laughs so hard that he tilts to one side. (Which he often does.)

YOUR BEST INVENTION
(SO FAR)

You've dreamed up some great inventions in this book. Draw your favorite one here.

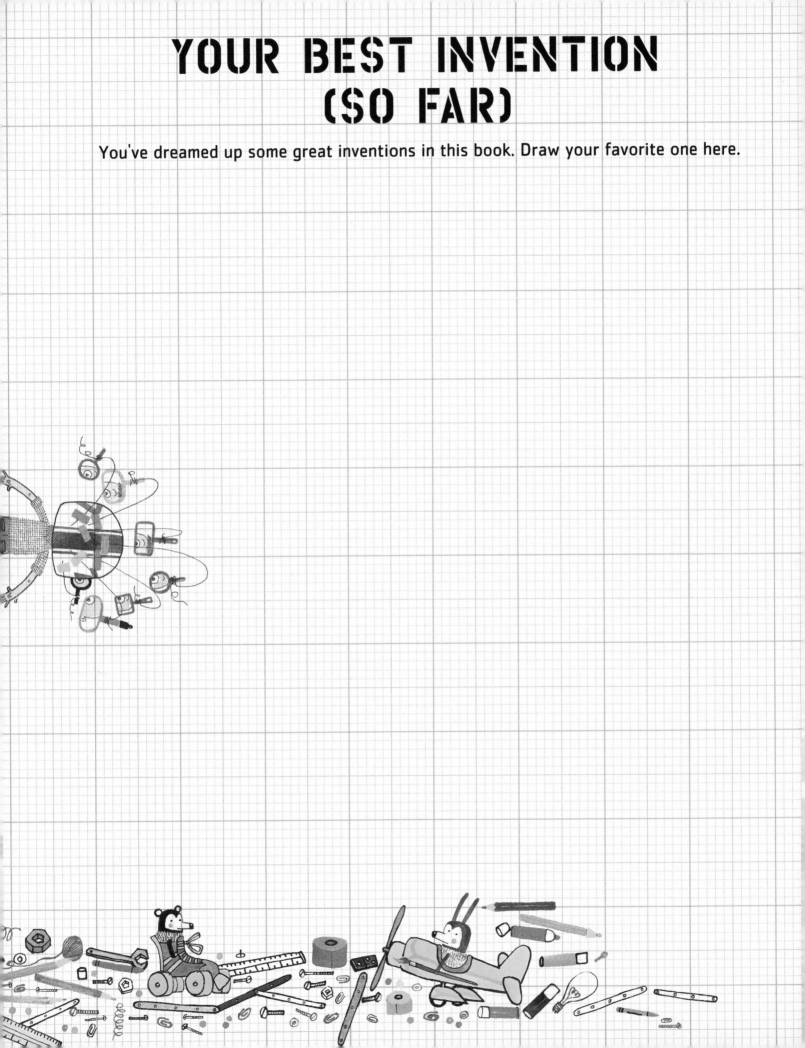

STORY TIME!

Creativity is essential for engineers. It lets them look at problems in new ways.
Writing a story is a great way to exercise your imagination.

Write a story about an engineering adventure you'd like to have one day.

MAKE YOUR MARK

Professional engineers use special stamps to identify their work.

Rosie has her own stamp of approval. Can you create your own stamp?

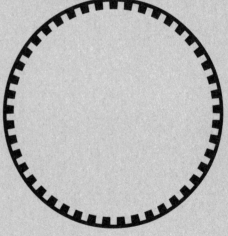

YOU'RE AN ENGINEER!

Make big plans here:

SOLUTION TO ENGINEER'S WORD SEARCH

B	T	R	A	N	S	P	O	R	T	A	T	I	O	N	J	R	Z	R	C	T	T	S	Y	S	T	E	M	S	R	I	N	B
I	G	F	S	G	I	N	D	U	S	T	R	I	A	L	E	N	S	A	G	R	I	C	U	L	T	U	R	A	L	S	U	L
O	A	E	A	U	T	O	M	O	T	I	V	E	S	M	E	C	H	A	T	R	O	N	I	C	A	K	T	T	O	L	A	V
M	P	R	T	R	M	A	N	U	F	A	C	T	U	R	I	N	G	J	L	M	C	N	S	S	K	O	K	E	A	C	S	E
E	O	K	C	I	T	O	P	T	I	C	A	L	Q	I	W	J	Y	A	F	Q	H	K	M	I	Q	M	K	C	I	R	R	I
D	W	Q	E	H	O	M	L	E	E	N	V	I	R	O	N	M	E	N	T	A	L	V	M	G	Q	U	I	G	E	A	U	U
I	E	M	L	A	I	A	H	S	T	R	U	C	T	U	R	A	L	C	O	M	P	U	T	E	R	N	R	E	W	P	X	Q
C	R	U	E	W	K	T	N	I	E	R	W	A	Y	E	V	I	M	O	F	U	U	H	N	H	A	U	N	T	P	U	O	L
A	W	P	C	E	J	K	E	M	N	A	O	Z	A	C	O	U	S	T	I	C	A	L	N	H	L	I	F	V	X	K	F	H
L	M	Z	T	P	R	V	S	C	I	O	U	L	G	Y	D	K	M	C	J	I	P	P	C	L	G	O	L	S	Y	R	T	V
Y	T	C	R	R	K	D	K	S	T	N	C	H	E	M	I	C	A	L	I	V	D	E	A	N	S	T	H	E	R	M	A	L
L	P	B	O	Y	I	O	R	Z	R	U	I	K	O	U	D	K	J	U	P	I	M	T	E	J	M	X	R	V	U	J	O	K
Q	Q	V	N	N	U	C	L	E	A	R	R	N	Q	A	M	W	K	W	E	L	E	O	C	S	K	M	Q	E	R	B	G	T
V	E	I	I	Q	M	R	A	I	B	Y	B	A	G	M	A	R	I	N	E	M	N	E	A	E	R	O	S	P	A	C	E	S
A	A	U	C	X	G	G	R	E	M	U	M	D	L	M	Y	D	B	F	N	A	R	I	V	E	R	F	L	V	S	N	Y	Z
Y	U	B	S	P	J	V	E	L	E	C	T	R	I	C	A	L	R	I	N	U	M	A	T	E	R	I	A	L	S	D	A	N

ACOUSTICAL	COMPUTER	MECHANICAL	PETROLEUM
AEROSPACE	ELECTRICAL	MECHATRONIC	RIVER
AGRICULTURAL	ELECTRONICS	METALLURGICAL	SOFTWARE
ARCHITECTURAL	ENVIRONMENTAL	MINING	STRUCTURAL
AUTOMOTIVE	INDUSTRIAL	NANOENGINEERS	SYSTEMS
BIOMEDICAL	MANUFACTURING	NUCLEAR	THERMAL
CHEMICAL	MARINE	OPTICAL	TRANSPORTATION
CIVIL	MATERIALS	POWER